SCOOBY-DOO!

An Even or Odd Mystery

THE CASE OF THE
ODDZILLA

by
Mark Weakland

illustrated by
Scott Gross

CAPSTONE PRESS
a capstone imprint

Published in 2015 by Capstone Press
A Capstone Imprint
1710 Roe Crest Drive
North Mankato, Minnesota 56003
www.capstonepub.com

Library of Congress Cataloging-in-Publication Data
Weakland, Mark, author.
Scooby-Doo! an even or odd mystery : the case of the oddzilla /
by Mark Weakland ; illustrated by Scott Gross.
pages cm. — (Solve It with Scooby-Doo! : math)
Summary: "The popular Scooby-Doo and the Mystery Inc. gang teach kids all about even and
odd numbers"— Provided by publisher.
Audience: Age 5–7.
Audience: Grades K to 3.
ISBN 978-1-4914-1541-2 (library binding)
1. Numbers, Natural—Juvenile literature. 2. Scooby-Doo (Fictitious character)—Juvenile
literature. I. Gross, Scott, illustrator. II. Title. III. Title: Case of the oddzilla.
QA141.3.W43 2015
513—dc23   2014002362

Editor: Shelly Lyons
Designer: Lori Bye
Art Director: Nathan Gassman
Production Specialist: Charmaine Whitman
The illustrations in this book were created digitally.

Thanks to our adviser for his expertise, research, and advice:
Jean B. Nganou, PhD
Department of Mathematics
University of Oregon

Printed in the United States of America in North Mankato, Minnesota.
032014   008087CGF14

A huge monster was chomping and stomping through Crystal Cove. Citizens were on edge. The police were stumped. But they knew they could call Scooby-Doo and the gang.

4

"It's eating things!" cried Chief Hammer. "There were 10 pins in the bowling lane at Big B's Bowl. Now there are 7. There were 6 matching hair dryers in the Clips and Snips Beauty Salon. Now there are 5. And there were 4 toy trucks in little Billy's backyard. Now there's only 1!"

Fred thought for a moment. "10 bowling pins, 6 hair dryers, and 4 trucks," he said. "They're all even numbers."

"And 7, 5, and 1 are odd numbers!" chimed in Velma.

"Maybe Shaggy is the monster," said Daphne. "There was an even number of doughnuts in your box. Now the number is odd!"

"A set contains an even number of objects if the objects can be matched. Look at the 8 forks. Each fork has a partner. There are 4 pairs. And look at the 10 spoons. Each spoon is matched with another. There are 5 pairs," said Fred.

Daphne put another fork down.
"Now it's even again. Shaggy and
Scooby—stay away from the trap!"

Oddzilla was hot on Scooby's trail. Scooby bolted down the street, straight toward the trap.

Oddzilla stopped and roared when it saw the objects. Then it clomped forward. Its jaws opened and closed. When it stepped on the plate, Fred pushed the button. Electricity sizzled. Oddzilla swayed then fell over with a loud clank.

Suddenly, a man ran out from behind a bush. "Oddzilla," he cried. "My beautiful creation!"

The chief stepped up and handcuffed the man.

I recognize that guy! It's Dan Ro. He's the creator of the You-Lost-One-I-Have-One web site. It's a company that sells single objects to people with unmatched sets.

Now that Oddzilla was gone, Scooby and Shaggy were thinking about better things—like pizza. The gang headed toward the restaurant.

"Like, Scoob, we never did get our pizza," said Shaggy.

"Rizza!" said Scooby.

"I think we all could go for a quick snack," said Fred.

Glossary

even number—a counting number that can be reached counting by 2 starting from 0

meddling—busying oneself with something that is not one's concern

odd number—a counting number that is not even; an odd number is one more than an even number

pair—a set of 2

set—a collection of well defined objects

veer—to change direction suddenly

Internet Sites

FactHound offers a safe, fun way to find Internet sites related to this book. All of the sites on FactHound have been researched by our staff.

Here's all you do:

Visit www.facthound.com

Type in this code: 9781491415412

Super-cool stuff! Check out projects, games and lots more at www.capstonekids.com